# GOOGLE CLOUD PROFESSIONAL COLLABORATION ENGINEER EXAM PRACTICE QUESTIONS & DUMPS

## EXAM STUDY GUIDE FOR PROFESSIONAL COLLABORATION ENGINEER EXAM PREP LATEST VERSION

**Presented By: Quantic Books**

## About Quantic Books:

Quantic Books is a publishing house based in Princeton, New Jersey, USA. , a platform that is accessible online as well as locally, which gives power to educational content, erudite collection, poetry & many other book genres. We make it easy for writers & authors to get their books designed, published, promoted, and sell professionally on worldwide scale with eBook + Print distribution. Quantic Books is now distributing books worldwide.

**Note:** Find answers of the questions at the last of the book.

## QUESTION 1

Your corporation has an OU that consists your sales team and an OU that consists your market research team. The sales team is frequently a target of mass email from authentic senders, which is distracting to their job responsibilities. The market research team also gets that email content, but they want it for the reason that it frequently consists interesting market analysis or competitive intelligence. Constant Contact is frequently used as the source of these messages. Your corporation also uses Constant Contact for your own mass email marketing. You must set email controls at the Sales OU without moving your own outgoing email or the market research OU.
What must you do?

A.  Make a blocked senders list as the Sales OU that consists the mass email sender addresses, but bypass this setting for Constant Contact emails.

B.  Make a blocked senders list at the root level, and then an sanctioned senders list at the Market Research OU, both comprising the mass email sender addresses.

C.  Make a blocked senders list at the Sales OU that consists the mass email sender addresses.

D.  Make an approved senders list at the Market Research OU that consists the mass email sender addresses.

## QUESTION 2

Your corporation has gotten help desk calls from clients about a new interface in Gmail that they had not seen before. They determined that it was a new feature that Google released in recent times. In the future, you'll need time to review the new features so you can accurately train workers before they see changes.

What action must you take?

A.  Corporation Profile > Profile > New Client Features > Permit "Scheduled Release"

B.  Apps > G Suite > Gmail > Uncheck "Permit Gmail Labs for my clients"

C.  Corporation Profile > Profile > New Client Features > Permit "Rapid Release"

D.  Device Management > Chrome > Device Settings > Stop auto-updates

## QUESTION 3

Your corporation frequently appoints from five to ten interns for short contract engagements and makes use of the same generically named G Suite accounts (e.g., client1@your-corporation.com, client2@your-corporation.com, client3@your-corporation.com). The manager of this program wants all email to these accounts routed to the manager's mailbox account also.

What must you do?

A. Setup address forwarding in each account's GMail setting menu.
B. Set up recipient address mapping in GMail Advanced Settings.
C. Arrange an Inbound Gateway route.
D. Give the manager delegated access to the mailboxes.

## QUESTION 4

Your-corporation.com in recent times bought 2500 Chrome devices and wants to distribute them to numerous crews globally. You decided that firm enrollment would be the best way to enforce corporation policies for managed Chrome devices. You discovered that Chrome devices presently end up in the top-level organization unit, and this needs to change to the organizational unit of the device administrator.

What must you do?

A. Change Enrollment Permissions to only allow clients in this organization to re-enroll existing devices.
B. Change Enrollment Controls to Place Chrome device in client organization.
C. Change Enrollment Controls to Keep Chrome device in current location.
D. Change Enrolment Permissions to not allow clients in this organization to enroll new devices.

## QUESTION 5

Your corporation in recent times transferred to G Suite and wants to deploy a commonly used third-party app to all of finance. Your OU structure in G Suite is broken down by subdivision. You must ensure that the accurate clients get this app.

What must you do?

A. For the Finance OU, permit the third-party app in SAML apps.
B. For the Finance OU, permit the third-party app in Marketplace Apps.
C. At the root level, disable the third-party app. For the Finance OU, allow clients to install any application from the G Suite Marketplace.
D. At the root level, disable the third-party app. For the Finance OU, allow clients to install only whitelisted apps from the G Suite Marketplace.


## QUESTION 6

The CEO of your corporation has indicated that messages from trusted contacts are being delivered to spam, and it is significantly moving their work. The messages from these contacts have not always been classified as spam. Additionally, you in recent times arranged SPF, DKIM, and DMARC for your domain. You have been tasked with troubleshooting the issue.

What two actions must you take? (Choose two.)

A. Obtain the message header and analyze using G Suite Toolbox.
B. Review the contents of the messages in Google Vault.
C. Set up a Gmail routing rule to whitelist the sender.
D. Conduct an Email log search to trace the message route.
E. Authenticate that your domain is not on the Spamhaus blacklist.


## QUESTION 7

Security and Compliance has recognized that data is being leaked

through a third-party application connected to G Suiteю You want to

investigate using an audit log. What log must you use?

A. Admin audit log
B. SAML audit log
C. Drive usage audit log
D. OAuth Token audit log

## QUESTION 8

A corporation has thousands of Chrome devices and bandwidth
restrictions. They want to distribute the Chrome device updates over a
period of days to avoid traffic spikes that would impact the low
bandwidth network.

Where must you permit this in the Chrome management settings?

A. Randomly scatter auto-updates.
B. Update over cellular.
C. Disable Auto update.
D. Throttle the bandwidth.

## QUESTION 9

Your corporation moved to G Suite last month and wants to install Hangouts Meet Hardware in all of their conference rooms. This will allow workers to walk into a room and use the in-room hardware to easily join their scheduled meeting. A distributed training session is coming up, and the facilitator wants to make remote room joining even easier. Participants in remote rooms must walk into their room and begin receiving the training without having to take any actions to join the session.

How must you accomplish this?

A. In the Admin Console, select the devices in Meeting Room Hardware, select Call, and Enter the meeting code.
B. Room participants will must start the meeting from the remote in the room.
C. By adding the rooms to the Calendar invite, they will all auto-join at the scheduled time.
D. Select Add Live Stream to the Calendar invite; all rooms added to the event will auto-join at the scheduled time.

## QUESTION 10

You are supporting an investigation that is being conducted by your litigation team. The current default retention policy for mail is 180 days, and there are no custom mail retention policies in place. The litigation team has identified a client who is central to the investigation, and they want to investigate the mail data related to this client without the client's awareness.

What two actions must you take? (Choose two.)

A. Move the client to their own Organization Unit, and set a custom retention policy
B. Make a matter using Google Vault, and share the matter with the litigation team members.
C. Make a hold on the client's mailbox in Google Vault
D. Reset the client's password, and share the new password with the litigation team.
E. Copy the client's data to a secondary account.

## QUESTION 11

Your Accounts Payable subdivision is auditing software license contracts corporation wide and has asked you to give a report that shows the number of active and suspended clients by organization unit, which has been set up to match the Regions and Subdivisions within your corporation. You must produce a Google Sheet that shows a count of all active client accounts and suspended client accounts by Org unit.

What must you do?

A. From the Admin Console Billing Menu, turn off auto-assign, and then click into Assigned Clients and export the data to Sheets.
B. From the Admin Console Clients Menu, download a list of all Clients to Google Sheets, and join that with a list of ORGIDs pulled from the Reports API.
C. From the G Suite Reports Menu, run and download the Accounts Aggregate report, and export the data to Google Sheets.
D. From the Admin Console Clients Menu, download a list of all client info columns and presently selected columns.


## QUESTION 12

You have arranged your G Suite account on the scheduled release track to give additional time to prepare for new product releases and determine how they will impact your clients. There are some new features on the latest roadmap that your director needs you to test as soon as they become generally available without changing the release track for the entire organization.

What must you do?

A. Make a new OU and tum on the rapid release track just for this OU.
B. Make a new Google Group with test clients and permit the rapid release track.
C. Establish a separate Dev environment, and set it to rapid release.
D. Ask Google for a demo account with beta access to the new features.

**QUESTION 13**

You are using Google Cloud Directory Sync to manage clients. You performed an initial sync of nearly 1,000 mailing lists to Google Groups with Google Cloud Directory Sync and now are planning to manage groups directly from Google. Over half the groups have been arranged with inaccurate settings, including who can post, who can join, and which groups can have external members. You must update groups to be arranged accurately.

What must you do?

A. Use the bulk upload with CSV feature in the G Suite Admin panel to update all Groups.
B. Update your configuration file and resync mailing lists with Google Cloud Directory Sync.
C. Make and assign a custom admin role for all group owners so they can update settings.
D. Use the Groups Settings API to update Google Groups with desired settings.

**QUESTION 14**

In your organization, clients have been provisioned with either G Suite Firm, G Suite Business, or no license, depending on their job responsibilities, and the cost of client licenses is paid out of each division's budget. In order to effectively manage the license disposition, team leaders require the ability to look up the type of license that is presently assigned, along with the last logon date, for their direct reports.

You have been tasked with recommending a solution to the Director of

- IT, and have gathered the following requirements: Team leaders

  needs to be able to retrieve this data on their own (i.e., self-service).
- Team leaders are not permitted to have any level of administrative
- access to the G Suite Admin panel. Team leaders needs to only be able to look up data for their direct reports.
- The data needs to always be current to within 1 week. Costs needs
- to be mitigated.

What approach must you recommend?

A. Export log data to BigQuery with custom scopes.

B. Use a third-party tool.

C. Use App Script and filter views within a Google Sheet.

D. Make an app using AppMaker and App Script.

## QUESTION 15

Your organization has been on G Suite Firm for one year. In recent times, an admin turned on public link sharing for Drive files without permission from security. Your CTO wants to get better insight into changes that are made to the G Suite environment. The chief security officer wants that data brought into your existing SIEM system.

What are two ways you must accomplish this? (Choose two.)

A. Use the Data Export Tool to export admin audit data to your existing SIEM system
B. Use Apps Script and the Reports API to export admin audit data to your existing SIEM system.
C. Use Apps Script and the Reports API to export drive audit data to the existing SIEM system
D. Use the BigQuery export to send admin audit data to the existing SIEM system via custom code
E. Use the BigQuery export to send drive audit data to the existing SIEM system via custom code.

## QUESTION 16

The executive team for your corporation has an comprehensive retention policy of two years in place so that they have access to email for a longer period of time. Your COO has found this useful in the past but when they went to find an email from last year to prove details of a contract in dispute, they were unable to find it. itis no longer in the Trash. They have requested that you recover it.

What must you do?

A. Using Vault, perform a search for the email and export the content to a standard format to give for investigation.
B. Using the Gmail Audit log, perform a search for the email, export the results, then import with G Suite Migration for Microsoft Outlook.
C. Using the Message ID, contact Google G Suite support to recover the email, then import with G Suite Migration for Microsoft Outlook.
D. Using the Vault Audit log, perform a search for the email, export the results. then import with G Suite Migration for Microsoft Outlook.

## QUESTION 17

In the years prior to your organization moving to G Suite, it was relatively common practice for clients to make consumer Google accounts with their corporate email address (for example, to monitor Analytics, manage AdSense, and collaborate in Docs with other partners who were on G Suite.) You were able to address active workers' use of consumer accounts during the rollout, and you are now concerned about blocking former workers who could potentially still have access to those services even though they don't have access to their corporate email account.
What must you do?

A. Contact Google Firm Support to give a list of all accounts on your domain(s) that access non-G Suite Google services and have them blocked.

B. Use the Transfer Tool for Unmanaged Accounts to send requests to the former clients to transfer their account to your domain as a managed account.

C. Give a list of all active workers to the managers of your corporation's Analytics, AdSense, etc. accounts, so they can clean up the respective access control lists.

D. Provision former client accounts with Cloud Identity licenses, generate a new Google password, and place them in an OU with all G Suite and Other Google Services disabled.


## QUESTION 18

Your organization has implemented Single Sign-On (SSO) for the multiple cloud-based services it utilizes. During verification, one service indicates that access to the SSO giver cannot be accessed due to invalid information.

What must you do?

A. Verify the NameID Element in the SAML Response matches the Assertion Consumer Service (ACS) URL.

B. Verify the Audience Element in the SAML Response matches the Assertion Consumer Service (ACS) URL.

C. Verify the Subject attribute in the SAML Response matches the Assertion Consumer Service (ACS) URL.

D. Verify the Recipient attribute in the SAML Response matches the Assertion Consumer Service (ACS) URL.

## QUESTION 19

A client does not follow their usual sign-in pattern and signs in from an

unusual location. What type of alert is triggered by this event?

A. Suspicious mobile activity alert.
B. Suspicious login activity alert.
C. Leaked password alert.
D. Client sign-in alert.


## QUESTION 20

The application development team has come to you requesting that a
new, internal, domain-owned G Suite app be allowed to access Google
Drive APIs. You are presently restricting access to all APIs using
approved whitelists, per security policy. You must grant access for this
app.

What must you do?

A. Permit all API access for Google Drive.
B. Permit "trust domain owned apps" setting.
C. Add OAuth Client ID to Google Drive Trusted List.
D. Whitelist the app in the G Suite Marketplace.

**QUESTION 21**

Your corporation's Chief Information Security Officer has made a new policy where third-party apps must not have OAuth permissions to Google Drive. You must rearrange current settings to adhere to this policy.

What must you do?

A. Access the Security Menu> API Reference > disable all API Access.
B. Access the Security Menu > API Permissions > choose Drive and Disable All Access.
C. Access the Security Menu > API Permissions > choose Drive and Disable High Risk Access.
D. Access Apps > G Suite > Drive and Docs > Sharing Settings and disable sharing outside of your domain


**QUESTION 22**

How can you monitor increases in client reported Spam as identified by Google?

A. Review post-delivery activity in the Email logs.
B. Review client-reported spam in the Investigation Tool.
C. Review spike in client-reported spam in the Alert center.
D. Review post-delivery activity in the BigQuery Export.

## QUESTION 23

The CFO just notified you that one of their team members wire-transferred money to the wrong account for the reason that they gotten an email that appeared to be from the CFO. The CFO has given a list of all clients that may be responsible for sending wire transfers. The CFO also gave a list of banks the corporation sends wire transfers to. There are no external clients that must be requesting wire transfers. The CFO is working with the bank to resolve the issue and needs your help to ensure that this does not happen again.

What two actions must you take? (Choose two.)

A. Arrange objectionable content to reject messages with the words "wire transfer."
B. Verify that DMARC, DKIM, and SPF records are arranged accurately for your domain.
C. Make a rule requiring secure transport for all messages regarding wire transfers.
D. Add the sender of the wire transfer email to the blocked senders list.
E. Permit all admin settings in Gmail's safety > spoofing and verification.

## QUESTION 24

Your corporation is in the process of deploying Google Drive Firm for your sales organization. You have discovered that there are many unmanaged accounts across your domain. Your security team wants to manage these accounts moving forward.
What must you do?
A. Disable access to all "Other Services" in the G Suite Admin Console.
B. Use the Transfer Tool for unmanaged accounts to invite clients into the domain.
C. Use the Data Migration Service to transfer the data to a managed account.
D. Open a support ticket to have Google transfer unmanaged accounts into your domain.

## QUESTION 25

Your chief compliance officer is concerned about API access to organization data across different cloud vendors. He has tasked you with compiling a list of applications that have API access to G Suite data, the data they have access to, and the number of clients who are using the applications.

How must you compile the data being requested?

A. Review the authorized applications for each client via the G Suite Admin panel.
B. Make a survey via Google forms, and collect the application data from clients.
C. Review the token audit log, and compile a list of all the applications and their scopes.
D. Review the API permissions installed apps list, and export the list.

## QUESTION 26

Your organization syncs directory data from Active Directory to G Suite via Google Cloud Directory Sync. Clients and Groups are updated from Active Directory on an hourly basis. A client's last name and primary email address have to be changed. You must update the client's data.

What two actions must you take? (Choose two.)

A. Add the client's old email address to their account in the G Suite Admin panel.
B. Change the client's primary email address in the G Suite Admin panel.
C. Change the client's last name in the G Suite Admin panel.
D. Change the client's primary email in Active Directory.
E. Change the client's last name in Active Directory.

## QUESTION 27

Your CISO is concerned about third party applications becoming compromised and exposing G Suite data you have made available to them. How could you give granular insight into what data third party applications are accessing?

What must you do?

A. Make a report using the OAuth Token Audit Activity logs.
B. Make a report using the Calendar Audit Activity logs.
C. Make a report using the Drive Audit Activity logs.
D. Make a reporting using the API Permissions logs for Installed Apps.

## QUESTION 28

Your Security Officer ran the Security Health Check and found the alert that "Installation of mobile applications from unknown sources" was occurring. They have asked you to find a way to prevent that from happening.

Using Mobile Device Management (MDM), you must arrange a policy

that will not allow mobile applications to be installed from unknown

sources. What MDM configuration is needed to meet this requirement?

A. In the Application Management menu, arrange the whitelist of apps that Android and iOS devices are allowed to install.
B. In the Application Management menu, arrange the whitelist of apps that Android, iOS devices, and Active Sync devices are allowed to install.
C. In Android Settings, ensure that "Allow non-Play Store apps from unknown sources installation" is unchecked.
D. In Device Management > Setup > Device Approvals menu, arrange the "Requires Admin approval" option.

## QUESTION 29

After a recent transition to G Suite, helpdesk has gotten a high volume of password reset requests and cannot respond in a timely manner. Your manager has asked you to determine how to resolve these requests without relying on additional staff.

What must you do?

A. Make a custom Apps Script to reset passwords.
B. Use a third-party tool for password recovery.
C. Permit non-admin password recovery.
D. Make a Google form to submit reset requests.

## QUESTION 30

Your organization deployed G Suite Firm within the last year, with the support of a partner. The deployment was conducted in three stages: Core IT, Google Guides, and full organization. You have been tasked with developing a targeted ongoing adoption plan for your G Suite organization.

What must you do?

A. Use Google Guides to deliver ad-hoc training to all of their co-workers and reports.
B. Use Work Insights to gather adoption metrics and target your training exercises.
C. Use Reports APIs to gather adoption metrics and Gmail APIs to deliver training content directly.
D. Use a script to monitor Email attachment types and target clients that aren't using Drive sharing.

## QUESTION 31

Your corporation in recent times decided to use a cloud-based ticketing system for your customer care needs. You are tasked with rerouting email coming into your customer care address, customercare@your-corporation.com to the cloud platform's email address, your-corporation@cloudgiver.com. As a security measure, you have mail forwarding disabled at the domain level.

What must you do?

A. Make a mail contact in the G Suite directory that has an email address of your-corporation@cloudgiver.com
B. Make a rule to forward mail in the customercare@your-corporation.com mailbox to your-corporation@cloudgiver.com
C. Make a recipient map in the G Suite Admin console that maps customercare@your-corporation.com to your-corporation@cloudgiver.com
D. Make a content compliance rule in the G Suite Admin console to change route to your-corporation@cloudgiver.com


## QUESTION 32

Your business partner requests that a new custom cloud application be

set up to log in without having separate credentials. What is your

business partner required to give in order to proceed?

A. Service giver logout URL
B. Service giver ACS URL
C. Identity Giver URL
D. Service giver certificate

## QUESTION 33

Your organization has in recent times gone Google, but you are not syncing Groups yet. You plan to sync all of your Active Directory group objects to Google Groups with a single GCDS configuration.

Which scenario could require an alternative deployment strategy?

A. Some of your Active Directory groups have sensitive group membership.
B. Some of the Active Directory groups do not have owners.
C. Some of the Active Directory groups have members external to organization.
D. Some of the Active Directory groups do not have email addresses.


## QUESTION 34

Your corporation has just gotten a shipment of ten Chromebooks to be deployed across the corporation, four of which will be used by remote workers. In order to prepare them for use, you must register them in G Suite.

What must you do?

A. Turn on the Chromebook and press Ctrl+Alt+E at the login screen to begin firm enrollment.
B. In Chrome Management | Device Settings, permit Forced Re-enrollment for all devices.
C. Turn on the chromebook and log in as a Chrome Device admin. Press Ctrl+Alt+E to begin firm enrollment.
D. Instruct the workers to log in to the Chromebook. Upon login, the auto enrollment process will begin.

## QUESTION 35

All Human Resources workers at your corporation are members of the "HR Subdivision" Team Drive. The HR Director wants to enact a new policy to restrict access to the "Worker Compensation" subfolder stored on that Team Drive to a small subset of the team.

What must you do?

A. Use the Drive API to modify the permissions of the Worker Compensation subfolder.
B. Use the Drive API to modify the permissions of the individual files contained within the subfolder.
C. Move the contents of the subfolder to a new Team Drive with only the relevant team members.
D. Move the subfolder to the HR Director's MyDrive and share it with the relevant team members.

## QUESTION 36

Client A is a Basic License holder. Client B is a Business License holder. These two clients, along with many additional clients, are in the same organizational unit at the same corporation. When Client A attempts to access Drive, they receive the following error: "We are sorry, but you do not have access to Google Docs Editors. Please contact your Organization Administrator for access." Client B is not presented with the same error and accesses the service without issues.

How do you give access to Drive for Client A?

A. Select Client A in the Directory, and under the Apps section, check whether Drive and Docs is disabled. If so, permit it in the Client record.
B. In Apps > G Suite > Drive and Docs, select the organizational unit the clients are in and permit Drive for the organizational unit.
C. In Apps > G Suite, determine the Group that has Drive and Docs permitd as a service. Add Client A to this group.
D. Select Client A in the Directory, and under the Licenses section, change their license from Basic to Business to add the Drive and Docs service.

## QUESTION 37

Your corporation is deploying Chrome devices. You want to make sure the machine assigned to the worker can only be signed in to by that worker and no one else.

What two things must you do? (Choose two.)

A. Disable Guest Mode and Public Sessions.
B. Permit a Device Policy of Sign In Screen and add the worker email address.
C. Enroll a 2-Factor hardware key on the device using the worker email address.
D. Permit a Client Policy of Multiple Sign In Access and add just the worker email address.
E. Permit a Device Policy of Restrict Sign In to List of Clients, and add the worker email address.

## QUESTION 38

The organization has conducted and completed Security Awareness Training (SAT) for all workers. As part of a new security policy, workers who did not complete the SAT have had their accounts suspended. The CTO has requested to be notified of any accounts that have been re-permitd to ensure no one is in violation of the new security policy.

What must you do?

A. Permit "Suspicious login" rule - Other Recipients: CTO
B. Permit "Suspended client made active" rule - Other Recipients: CTO
C. Permit "Email settings changed" rule - -Other Recipients: CTO
D. Permit "Suspended client made active" rule and select "Deliver to" Super Administrator(s)

# ANSWER

1. **Correct Answer: A**
2. **Correct Answer: A**
3. **Correct Answer: C**
   **Reference:**
   https://support.google.com/a/answer/2685650?hl=en
4. **Correct Answer: A**
5. **Correct Answer: B**
   **Reference:**
   https://support.google.com/a/answer/6089179?hl=en
6. **Correct Answer: AC**
7. **Correct Answer: D**
   **Reference:**
   https://support.google.com/a/answer/6124308?hl=en
8. **Correct Answer: A**
   **Reference:**
   https://support.google.com/chrome/a/answer/3168106?hl=en
9. **Correct Answer: D**
10. **Correct Answer: DE**
11. **Correct Answer: D**
    **Reference:**
    https://support.google.com/a/answer/7348070?hl=en
12. **Correct Answer: A**
    **Reference:**
    https://support.google.com/a/answer/172177?hl=en
13. **Correct Answer: A**
14. **Correct Answer: C**
15. **Correct Answer: CE**
16. **Correct Answer: A**
17. **Correct Answer: C**
18. **Correct Answer: B**
    **Reference:** https://auth0.com/docs/protocols/saml/saml-
    configuration/troubleshoot/auth0-as-sp
19. **Correct Answer: B**
    **Reference:**
    https://support.google.com/a/answer/7102416?hl=en
20. **Correct Answer: C**
21. **Correct Answer: D**
    **Reference:**
    https://support.google.com/a/answer/60781?hl=en
22. **Correct Answer: C**

23. **Correct Answer: BD**
24. **Correct Answer: C**
25. **Correct Answer: A**
26. **Correct Answer: AC**
27. **Correct Answer: A**
28. **Correct Answer: C**
    Reference:
    https://support.google.com/a/answer/7491893?hl=en
29. **Correct Answer: C**
    Reference:
    https://support.google.com/a/answer/33382?hl=en
30. **Correct Answer: A**
31. **Correct Answer: B**
32. **Correct Answer: B**
    Reference:
    https://support.google.com/a/answer/6087519?hl=en
33. **Correct Answer: C**
34. **Correct Answer: A**
    Reference:
    https://support.google.com/chrome/a/answer/4600997?hl=en
35. **Correct Answer: B**
36. **Correct Answer: D**
37. **Correct Answer: BC**
38. **Correct Answer: D**